Arclight

John Biscello

Arclight
© 2019 John Biscello

All rights reserved.
Printed in the United States of America.

No part of this book may be used, stored in a system retrieval system, or transmitted, in any form or in any means – by electronic, mechanical, photocopying, recording, or reproduced in any manner whatsoever - without written permission from the author, except in the case of brief quotations embodied in critical articles and reviews.
For information, address Indie Blu(e) Publishing.
indieblucollective@gmail.com

Published in the United States of America by Indie Blu(e) Publishing

ISBN: 978-1-7328000-2-1
Library of Congress Control Number: 2019901472

Editors:
Kindra M. Austin
Christine E. Ray

Cover Art courtesy of Heather Ross

DEDICATION

For my families: both in Taos and New York.

Contents

Half-Light..1

Lighted Tatters...............................17

Brightening Light..........................37

Reflective Light..............................49

Unremembered to Light...............69

Arclight..79

Lighted Proof..............................109

Half-Light

John Biscello

Claim for the Meek

I do not want to see
the face of God.
I want to see her mask,
where
and for whom it cracked,
the causal history of lines and fissures,
want to trace,
with blind mute innocence,
the light quartered and drawn
in Braille, its grooves holding,
without strain or regret,
Mercy's hidden inheritance.

Immigration Laws

We are immigrants in our own skin,
flash-fire refugees
who get by with falsified papers,
fake IDs, and forged signatures.
If caught
and found guilty
of a trespass
or transgression,
we pardon ourselves
in our native tongues,
language a placeholder
for the names
we were forced
to annul.

John Biscello

Eden

It was no longer Eden,
but the bones of Eden.
They looked around, they glummed
and chimped, they moped and wondered.
Then what they did, ably penitent,
refugees in their own backyard,
they screwed to no avail. They
screwed and screwed, the strident
conjugation of the lonely and the damned,
tried to screw their way out of
and past the desert spleening blues,
tried to abolish Memory in briny paroxysms.
Was it like that?
A constant and necessary
giving and receiving of fire through flesh
and flinty roil?
Did the seeds pop and sputter
and spin like so many disco grains
among soil and waste?
It was no longer Eden,
but the bones of Eden.
Out of the dust
came the first ever
love letter between bodies
and husk.

Arclight

Apples

One turn of the hip,
upsetting the apple cart—
Eden after dark.

John Biscello

Meet Me at the End of the Tunnel

Forsaken angel
seeking Mortal reprieve—
Serious applicants only.

Begin

No need for the past,
living mythology, you,
here and now, begin.

John Biscello

Country

Your soul's country
is much bigger
than you think.
Find every last you
there.

Backroads

Traveling mapless backroads,
I found heaven
looking for me.

John Biscello

Pearl

She came from the sea,
she came to marvel the pearl's
pinkest let to grieve.

Ophelia's Blues

Her sad, sea-green dress,
an epitaph, rippling quietly,
as if in a dream.
The small history
of a fresh wraith,
white fingers forever
separating the bones
from the silt.

John Biscello

After Party

She, Lazarus,
back from the dead,
with a musical vengeance—
A beat, Christ, please,
she asks of her martyred D.J.,
half-light, half-man,
and out climbs her voice, grinding
through rubble, a dark velvet toy
wound up for centuries, released,
on behalf of every last blue girl, unannounced,
notes from underground
unfurling a cortege of white ribbons,
grace lost
now found
among trespasses.

Arclight

Lovesong, the Remix

It became a goal,
soul-mate to my own damned self—
Nerves on the first date.

John Biscello

Beacon

Early morning.
Turning to face you. First kiss, skin on skin,
to claim holy fire
coiled in mortal intimacy.
I know that one day I will die
to you, you to me, Time bruises softly.
Sense of ephemera
compels me to draw you closer,
to warm my hand on your cheek,
to say something, anything
to make you smile,
to ignite that beacon
in which I bask
silently grateful.
To savor, to cherish.
The hidden vocabulary
of my heart
is reduced to essentials,
its rowing simple and direct.
I love you.
There is no need to invent new words,
new modes of being,
when first kiss,
skin on skin,
renews itself
for the sake of Eden's ageless memory.

Minuet

Almost dusk. Young
unbridled lovers, hands bonded,
fingers chaste in a minuet,
lying on their backs in the
sun-spiked grass
of the graveyard.
The boy whispers something
into the girl's ear, the girl giggles
at that something, and then silence,
in which the epitaph marking love's tender passage,
is being written for future reference.

Lighted Tatters

John Biscello

Tango

Summer,
how butterflies tango
in upward-moving flux

Bask

Rapt, in gratitude,
the writer fasting on silence,
and slimmest wisps,
to gain Beauty's favor
and superlative bask,
beyond recognition.

John Biscello

Abscond

When, at last,
you have stripped
to the final comma
and pause, will form,
in its undue measures
and remittance, default
to the quiet sum of zero,
a grave claim
lightened
by a gradual shed?

Coil

To caper at the edge,
where the seething lyric
happens, poetry with slits
and fast teeth,
where the hours of phenomena
are boiled and reduced
to a single quivering instant,
an umbilical knot
of light
upon tenderest scraps
and coils.

John Biscello

Ravels

At the wound's core,
dark
luscious
ravels
of text,
courting,
inviolate measures,
the fathomless brood
of Beauty's End.

Tatters

For many years
I asked Grief to
wait outside my window,
a peripheral guest
chancing obscure, fugitive
details, and lighted tatters.
Have I been a poor host,
stranger to my own ghost
and remnants?

John Biscello

Tow

Is grace
not near grief,
a mirror's oblique run
of necessary doubles,
how we, with hearts in tow
to drift and slow bleed,
ask of tides
a lone dock
among so much sea.

Marvel

As a child,
the thinnest greenest
wisps of air
held
tiny totemic figures
of me,
carved from sheer terror,
aloft,
and I pretended,
O how I pretended
to be the biggest strongest
bravest boldest
of them all,
a clown-saint crossing
a tightrope on a unicycle
while juggling flaming balls
to the sound of thunderous applause
which kept me in the air
until the war outside my world
coming from the next room
broke in
reminding me
how very small I was
and I fell down
and away
from everything I longed to be

John Biscello

Funky Monk

Today was strange.
The sweet, quiet, solemn, solitary
monk
who lives in the cork-lined antechamber
inside me
was dancing.
This is not something I have ever seen him do.
I went to visit him,
expecting the usual: him
hunched over his mahogany desk,
pen in hand, eyes narrowed
hawk-like tracking the words that
bled black onto his parchment,
but this time I was shocked
when I entered to what could
only be described as monk-funk,
a check-a-chow-check-a-chow-wow-wow
blaxploitation guitar riff, backed by a sledgehammer
bass drum husbanded to cave temple chants,
and there was my monk, engaged in self-contained
spells of spastic bop, which soon flowered in range
and elasticity, his arms freewheeling Baptist-revival-style,
his sandaled feet doing the hot coal jitterbug,
and if all that wasn't strange enough,
my monk was wearing a purple three-piece suit,
the kind that stylistically crossed Prince with Dean Martin.
I was astonished.
This was unprecedented.
My monk
had lived inside
the cork-lined antechamber
inside me

Arclight

since forever,
and not once
had I seen him
wear anything but his brown robes,
nor had I ever seen him
bust a move of any sort.
He was not a move-busting monk,
he was a still and solitary one
who split most of his time
between scribbling on parchment
or meditatively pacing
around the room
staring at
or into the cork-lined walls
or at
or into
the bare floor,
but really those
were just impressionistic
reference points
for his staring
and dwelling deeper within
himself.
Once when I asked him
if he got lonely,
after all I was his only visitor,
and my visits were few and far between,
he smiled and said—*Happylonely*
and his crescent smile,
so sweet, so gentle,
made me want to cry.
My monk,
the happylonely, quiet, sweet, solitary
dude,

who, at this very moment, is standing on a chair,
rhythmically
pan gliding his index
right to left, his other hand slapping
thunder against his thigh as he shimmypops
from knees to chest.
I close the door
and leave my monk
to his impromptu getdown.
Dance motherfucker dance,
I hear him shout
to no one in particular.
I have never heard my monk curse,
nor speak three words in succession.
His radical behavior concerns me.
And excites my sense of wonder.
Does this mean
that the others
living inside me,
the ones whose behaviors and patterns
were regulated and predictable,
their methods of operation
habituated and specific,
does this mean
that they might start
transgressing expectations
and defying conventions
and acting differently?
In what ways
would they act different?
And what will that mean
for me
as their singular, host entity?
I return to the door

Arclight

of the antechamber
peer through the peephole
and see my monk
dancing freely
and wildly
amidst the parchment
that is now whirling
confetti-like around the room,
and I begin to understand
the true nature of revolution
just a tiny bit more
as I walk away from the door,
smiling,
happy to know
there's a dancing monk
who lives inside me.

John Biscello

I Believe in Miracles

I am learning,
or perhaps unlearning,
to believe wildly
in the fresh crop
and siege of miracles
that are happening
right under my eyes
every day.
If I fail to see them,
if my self-limiting perspective
narrows into a myopic squint,
that's on me,
and I shouldn't blame
the miracles
for my dearth of vision
and lack of imagination.
Outside,
an orange poppy
trembles
when drops of rain
kiss
and silver
its petals.
A child bumbles
along a carpet of fresh grass,
its cherubic face
lit up like a Mardi Gras
lantern
as she journeys newly
into the world of toddling.
A wrinkled hand,
roped in vines

Arclight

of blue veins,
clasps
another vine-veined hand,
husband and wife
of sixty-four years,
this simple gesture of
you are my home
repeated over and through
many moons, laughs,
and tears.
Gulls bop-ambling along a shoreline
as a fish mongering choir,
the thousand broken azure
fingers of the sea
reaching toward
a glittering bounty of washed-up shells,
clouds as wooly prayer beds
holding the incalculable breadth of God,
an anchored ballet of lotuses in a pond,
autumn winds turning stray leaves
into golden migrants,
stones nobly
carrying the true history of the world
in their gray silences,
the riotous joy of children
playing in the park,
a religion of its own
with no pulpit
or doctrine required,
that person
passing you in the street,
or standing next to you
in line at the supermarket,
who is you,

John Biscello

how they hurt
and struggle
and dream
and wonder
and worry and
grow scared
and want to be loved
just like you,
humanity
the simple common denominator
which is infinitely greater and richer
than the big-budget, whiz-bang
special effects, spectacle-scope,
my-religion-is-bigger-than-yours
form of miracles
that so many eyes
are turned toward,
breeding the skinned, reflective laments
that our souls, brute
in their divine, unrelenting wisdom
and foresight,
pose to us repeatedly
(sometimes
as inner screams,
sometimes as rippling whispers)
How much you missed today,
my love, there were miracles
everywhere,
right under your eyes, your nose,
at your fingertips,
but that's okay, today is today
and it's never too late
to embrace the wild gospel
of revolutionary seeing.

Arclight

I See Myself

I always saw the humanity
behind his thick-lidded eyes, the small child,
begging for a banquet of golden crumbs
to appease the motherache churning
in his heart and stomach.
A thousand lions
pitted against a studded
chain smoking beer gutted gladiator,
I saw that too, he, the lions, the gladiator,
the arena,
the smoke and booze,
all of it,
held hard in a concentrated siege,
a flash-flood and toxic smolder, and at his feet,
I cowered, and proceeded to bury myself.
He was my father,
still is. The bond between us thick
as viscous chains,
the sort that perpetrate magma,
and rattle and clank
when carried by the blue shivery breath
of ghosts
down long hallways
branching out
into labyrinths
where every last bruised nothing
meets to forge bonds.
We are there, partly,
he and I, father and son,
but also, I am here,
a rampant indwelling,
a man who learned to take a saw

John Biscello

to chains,
warbling
heavy metal into blues,
a nightingale, moon throated, with laryngitis,
yes, it is never too soon
or late to sing,
and I, in my mortal remains,
exist as living proof,
I am here, mostly,
a boy, a man,
the ghosts
no longer my enemies,
nor the bared teeth of an infant haunt,
but rather my teachers, my guides,
and when I look into his eyes,
I see staggered humanity, a small child,
a human doing the best he can,
I see myself, expanding
beyond the myth of lions
and gladiators,
I see myself,
rapt and sealed,
signing my name
to soul,
and blessed to know
Beauty's lasting friendship.

Arclight

Autobiography

To know myself,
a rogue aggregate
of loving atoms,
a happy shivering clusterfuck
of luminous baubles
banded together
to forge and assume
an alleged identity,
no papers or pulpit required,
to fulfill an arc, and heart-guided directives,
to be a kid, with a hymn-book,
and the keys to the kingdom,
for God knows how long,
then dispersion,
back to the warm bath
of light and sound,
and I
will no longer be I,
and though breaking up
is hard to do,
and this will be by far
the most challenging break-up
in my life,
I, me-less, will depart,
lightly, without going anywhere,
soul at play, lidless
in its capacity to contain grief
and love.

Brightening Light

John Biscello

I Do Not Say

I do not say I love you,
but I notice how your fingers
twine and wrap around empty,
tracing broken circles in the air
when you are nervous.
I do not say I love you,
but there is a spot on the nape of your neck,
which radiates blush with the slightest tease
or provocation, and I do not tell you
how I belong to it,
its small history, and wisps of symmetry
soldering pink to gasp.
I do not say I love you,
Silence, you see, my longstanding master,
having taught me the gauzy reckon
of slow holy burn,
and ice floes, papered with daisies,
adrift in motherless golden haze,
perpetrating nature as silent cinema
with lines and actors to spare.
I do not say I love you,
but I know all of your hiding places,
and have left bread-crumbs there to commemorate
your movements between revelation and secrecy.
I do not say I love you,
for there are words, unborn, wanting, waiting,
wanting, hard-pressed to become
rose blood on vellum edges,
pinches brightening subtle measures
and violent pauses.
I do not say I love you,
but I dutifully observe and record

Arclight

every starred recognition,
turning the world on its ear,
tracing my mouth to the air that your hands
just touched then abandoned.
I do not say I love you,
but I do not forget, ever.
Memory, exact in its tether
to origins, shows me
a home,
a harbor,
an exchange to marry music
to breath in frets and starts.
I do not say I love you,
my voice, time-locked to nuance,
finds you again and again
in poems,
bound between the cross-hairs
of absence
and praise.

John Biscello

I Listen

Dawn. The sea breeze,
salt-fringed, rolls in through
the opened glass doors,
its damp fingers sifting
and touching upon
the cravings,
rent and folds
of our shared bare skin,
It's like home, you say,
and this makes me dig my nails
in deeper,
like a feral cat, just learning
how to regulate and express its affection
through its claws,
Like a poem, is what you say next,
and I lay my head on your chest
and stay there
no longer the boy I was
the one who used to be terrified
of hearts,
ones belonging to others,
my own,
something about the beating
freaked me out, i.e.,
when I'd place my hand
over my own heart
I couldn't bear it
it felt too powerful
too real
too something
and I'd quickly withdraw
to spare myself both the cause

Arclight

and effect.
I am not that boy anymore.
I let my head stay on your chest,
your breathing a lullaby-raft
upon which I feel safe and secure,
held, and soothed to no end,
I allow my ear to openly receive
the music of your heart, its rabbit-beatings,
I listen, when you tell me this is all there is, I listen, when you giggle
at my off-color remarks
involving salt, dust, bones,
honey, and you,
I listen,
when you laugh
at my riff on junkie clowns
staring down nostalgic maraschino sunsets,
and when I ask you
to tell me something good,
something sweet,
and you speak my name, three times, softly,
I listen,
then watch
as you begin to cry,
from open wounds,
soundlessly.

John Biscello

Cherish

This side of dream,
to marvel in sheer trespass
and longing,
to engage the mystery
and riot of skin,
by touch
and flagrant cherish.

Sunder

To leave
sheer vowels
and sudden clefts upon the warm, dream-wet
infinity of skin,
so wherever she goes,
whenever,
sundered verses
will marvel as placeholders.

John Biscello

Braille

Touch,
how her body
becomes a pulsing
slate of Braille,
your fingers, unfinished,
running on

Arclight

Sublime

The mouth,
birthing a migrant kiss,
begs gravity's pardon
in raising lips
to a sublime arc.

John Biscello

Slow Dancing for Beginners

It is not about holding her perfect,
just so, in a prescribed manner,
but rather, can you slowpour your breath
into one another's hips
and clefts, while swaying?
It is the mutual pressing
of scars together, a controlled
friction that teaches your hidden
wounds to sing, raising
the pitch of tender pink
to soprano, exploding shells
of outworn scabs
until the cadence is one of
melting. How to begin?
Take her hand,
lock your gaze with hers,
and simply ask: May I have this dance?
Music optional.

Arclight

Aria for Two Voices

It was perfect
in that our distances
mirrored one another's
fragile attempts for
lasting intimacy,
and in reaching
we were guaranteed
to come up empty
yet singing.

Reflective Light

John Biscello

Isn't It Romantic?

Baby Byron didn't yet have language,
so he twisted and contorted
his face into a mask, a distressed aria
sounding his discomfort.
That it was existential, and not hunger, thirst,
tiredness, or physical pain, meant nothing
to him. Without language
as a stingy placeholder, the word Existential
was no more than a whiff of flatulence,
or evil wind stirring the mobile
of planets and stars above his head,
that he gawked at night after night,
amused by their rotation and melody.

He was, lately, gripped with an urge
to toddle from point A to B,
two-legged, as he had seen
Baby Blake do.
Baby Blake, angel-locked, always smelling
of sour milk and dandelions,
and gurgling verses that brushed against
Baby Byron's soft cheek like so many
wet feathers. Baby Wordsworth, he was a mouthful,
and he'd randomly strike Baby Byron on the head
with that rattley club he carried around.
Baby Wordsworth's fierce tactics
could bring hot to Baby Byron's face,
and water, stinging, slashed
pink on pink. If Baby Byron could
have found the words and made them
obey his tongue, he might have
expressed his utter contempt

Arclight

not only for Baby Blake and Baby Wordsworth,
but also for the imbecilic gestures
which he made, seemingly involuntarily.
There was a palsied, halting, jilted
quality to the things deep inside him
from which he demanded
grace and fluency.
Yet, despite his yearning, he shit himself.
Needed a running tap
of breast from which to draw.
If left on his back, as he frequently was
(planets, stars, round and round,
again and again, oh god, nausea)
he'd waggle his limbs
like an epileptic beetle.
Is this all there is, Baby Byron pondered,
not in words or language, but more of a pressure
just below his navel. Terror, awe,
and a mutable series of paroxysms?
Through the vertical slats, Baby Byron
could hear Baby Blake reciting an ode.
Or choking on a piece of small hard plastic.
It was hard to interpret Baby Blake.
Baby Byron shifted his attention
to the cosmic mobile. For the first time,
he noticed that one of the stars
was slightly darker than the others, a stain
setting it apart as unique. Pleased with his discovery,
Baby Byron claimed the dark star as his own,
his short reach
toward eternity
an awful row
and first word away.

John Biscello

Preschool, a Love Story

Jilly, aged three, bared her teeth
& bit Jack, four, hard on the arm, breaking skin &
drawing blood.
Stunned, Jack's baby blues
ballooned & gaped at Jilly,
bright with malice & glee.
Why Jilly why, Jack cried,
nursing his wound.
Cuz that's how much
I love you Jack, how much you
there is in me.
As Jilly picked Jack's skin
from her teeth, Jack's heart
turned into a pair of flying scissors
& cut Jilly's hidden paper doll
into a puddle of tiny pieces.
Matching wounds,
with grace & fidelity,
the two lovemates
embarked on their honeymoon
years before they were married.

The Argument

Reality and me
have disagreements all the time.
Reality is, by nature, inviolable.
And a bit of an existential bully.
I am, by illicit union, a child of fiction.
And tender in the center.
Reality and me don't always see eye to eye.
In the end reality always wins out,
but there's something
keenly touching
about being one's own best fanboy
in support of a cause
where victories are small
and loss
is the grail on order.

John Biscello

No Runway Required

How come
no one ever asks,
What are you
metaphysically
wearing right now?
Are you basking
in translucent skivvies,
rocking spangled self-awareness,
dream-dropping golden drawers
and grace-lace in multi-storied tatters,
are you so flagrantly naked right now,
candle-wax-drip in a homuncular beehive
on a Saturday night in heaven,
that you are rising, unleavened,
toward a new species of self-hood?
Are you clad in night-armor,
clank-stepping to the beat of your own private drummer?
Are you on fire, from the waist down? The neck up?
Is the tender, supple geography of your body
high-classing it three-piece-prayer style?
Is your invisible overcoat thick as chagrin
and molasses? Do you feel warm? Safe?
Sick of existential hand-me-downs
which come from another time, another place?
Who exactly is wearing pink bunny slippers
from the dustbin of memory,
fuzzy brown sweaters
loved to a state of sentimental holiness,
sleeveless hearts exposed to scarring
and sun?
We live in a world of private parts
and cyclical makeovers,

Arclight

and yet how rare it is
for someone to ask,
What are you metaphysically wearing
right now?

John Biscello

Tunnel

Consider the mole, a small
important god, unfettered
by dreams of flight
or fugitive arcs, gathering
briskly the dark into its labor,
leveling a dig
to assume no chances
or saviors

Drum

Drum over me
God, I am water
under the bridge,
threaded with silk
and sewn with bones
flowing,
undammed,
into the percussive
folds of a liquid body,
my name
and past
ceded
to babbles of foam
upon a colossal, quivering
crash of silence.

John Biscello

Graze

Clouds,
how we graze
upon the incalculable
breadth of God,
storm watch notwithstanding.

Arclight

Endanger

Savior,
how we endanger
mirrors without
further reflection.

John Biscello

Secrets

Keeping secrets
from yourself
is like talking behind
someone's front.

Arclight

Annul

Forgiveness,
gravity's claim
on cells
duly annulled.

John Biscello

Unabated

Hope,
that thing unfettered,
soul's window flung open,
to bask, to air myself,
unabated, no past
to claim
or follow.

Arclight

Palms

Mercy Street runs lengthwise
to the sun. Its soul,
to orient, turns its nearest cheek
to flaring palms.

John Biscello

Palmistry

Eternity,
misconceived as a noun,
and now?
My palms stay open all night.

Arclight

Ink

Devotion,
the day you ink
small miracles
in a palm
not your own.

John Biscello

Disclosure

In perpetual flirtation
and basking courtship
with Beloved,
I, warming to petition
and gospel,
humbly sign my name,
if only to ghost an echo
channeling undisclosed remains.

Unremembered to Light

John Biscello

Arson

To speak fire
these days, to claim
desire in a fierce consumptive
manner, is no longer a popular notion,
no longer in vogue. It is an outworn,
outmoded, outdated form of expression.
We know too much,
we know too much about the brain, its bio-chemical feeds
and chains,
know too much about disorders,
dysfunctions, and behavioral range,
we have cased the bomb-shelters
and burned—put hovels in which
our inner children live, wrestle,
wrangle, and mate,
we know too much
to risk in words—
I want to possess you,
be possessed by you—
the talk of angels
and Neruda-speak
are no longer aural emblems
of deeply dreamed longing,
but rather implications
that qualify one for
unhealthy dependency
(i.e., We present to you Exhibit B).
Souls can no longer burn
freely, like dumb primal
wildfires, love has become too
smart, it knows too much
about itself, its causes and effects;

Arclight

to speak fire
is a cranial threat, an admission replete
with its own keys and warden, but to not speak it
is a death for those who still believe
in tongues
and words
as clumsy attempts
at impossible measures.

John Biscello

Pour

This is how I grieve—
words, pearlescent
to glean, and bare,
poured,
like so much light,
on petals
bruised by touch
and Beauty rare.

Indelible

To ebb,
the startling clarity
of a stolen kiss
sentenced to null
and ghost, to lips
indelibly parted
then closed.

John Biscello

Thorns

Blossom,
hue of vetted contradiction,
between cherish and fade—
Hours, like thorns, slow burn
to chasten.

Arclight

Crescendo

What about
the rough, thorny grace
of angels locked in love-play,
the traceless sex of light piercing light,
scaling an impossible crescendo?

John Biscello

Gist

The manic blush
and titter of young love
is no serum
nor mirage,
but rather the gist of bloom
martyred so soon
to thorns.

Arclight

Winter, a Love Story

Winter's brides,
wearing long white scarves of sleet and song,
touching pale sky to blue lips,
breathing memory and frost,
their sorrow
and spectral want
grows hands
that enclose me, a robust crush,
matrimonial in its grip,
until I am no more than a whiff of air,
and then, not even that, a traceless speck
unremembered to light,
and how it falls.

Arclight

John Biscello

God's Word Against Mine

And on the eighth day
she was diagnosed an Artist,
and saw that it was good
and fierce and necessary,
and went forth creating
like a madwoman,
rattling gravity shackles
to the din of furor
and crumbling towers
within.

Arclight

Anne Sexton

It begins with a stopwatch, and a glass of water.
The stopwatch belonged to her father, or to her father's father.
The glass of water is a joke. Imagine trying to remedy
all that desert within, all that scabbing red sand blown, with a
single glass of water.
No, Anne, your dry heaves ran deep, your mirages coercions
shivering like wet sheets of plasma. The eye could only see so
far,
the confessions could only cart you a dash further than the eye's
migration,
and where you left off, you began to teeter, and veer, to gag on
green wind.
In the fairy tale, you were the witch, with seaweed for hair, and
the daughter,
the red-hooded little girl with a broken stopwatch functioning as
a false talisman:
time was not on your side, it climbed all over you and clung
like co-dependent parasites on parade, and you writhed in agony,
cried out for your father, before lying down and falling asleep on
the forest-bed of pines.
When you awoke, the world was white, new-white, clean-white,
too-clean-white,
scary-glaring,
and there was the blurred transit of hands, hooks, smocks,
scrubs, operating instructions,
soft voices like slippered footsteps on carpeted stairs,
a mounting turban of verdigris bandages.
None of it made sense. You did the best you could,
you stood up, you sat down, you confessed, as if every word was
a grain of sand spitballed
into the eye of Eternity, you crafted a swimming hole in your
desert

John Biscello

and brought lovers there to soak with you.
The sun kept on, as did time, wind, pills, angels,
you sang through your wounds, daily,
your typewriter a pet from heaven, which you ribbon-fed scaly
bits of hell.
It went on, and on, until it didn't, the angels scattering all at
once,
or perhaps reshuffling to gather and lift you up.
It ends with a stopwatch, locked in a drawer,
and an empty glass, where water
once touched lips.

Arclight

Sylvia Plath

To be a mother, and to double as a dark sorceress, a cleaver of dried bones, could not have been easy. Especially in the 1950s. They burned witches then, as well as reds and blacks and faggots, and other things that didn't fit the paradigmatic slant. It was a time of burning, though televisions were new, and lawns were green and sprinklered, and men chewed cud while shaving their second faces. Also, they burned witches way back when, and now too, it seems witch-hunts belong to some fraternal order of treason, some moose club with crooked antlers, who knows.

You wrote poems. No, you fevered them. Red-hot blues, peppered shards of black. You held bits of the moon hostage, or she you. You mooned for the world, a she-wolf's strip-tease, straight to the bone, and also, also there was your death's head vaudeville act, juggling scythes, gargling ram's blood and spitting it back out as flames that burned skyward, charring the fluffed bellies of clouds.

Alchemy, vaudeville, burlesque, spells brightening hollowed veins and inflaming corpuscles, spells animating petrified, rotting limbs, Lady Lazarus with a sideways grin, you did it all, Miss Plath, and still had time to make dinner. Still took care of the kids. Doing all these things while crossing the River Styx on a paper boat must not have been easy. But the poems, papered heartbeats, glistening with sap and resin, as if torn directly from dream-womb, and left behind for us to ponder, digest, fill our bathtubs with and swim in.

Your silver, vagabond, winter-kissed drops, pressed between the margins of an unyielding sea, will not be forgotten, for the moon holds the tides accountable for all its parceled beauty.

John Biscello

Emily Dickinson

At the severest hour, everything fell within.
A banquet hall after the crash, after the deluge, and you,
a mouse, courting lull, tracked paw prints in flour,
stalking floorboards for crumbled manna.
You, the mouse, with slow heaven firing your eyes,
appraising the mess, and determined to put the house back in
order.
Sure, it was a tall task for a meek creature,
but you had stilted symmetry and angelic stutters on your side,
they were your virtues and allegiances, and so, approximating
in soul fingered shorthand, in radical glyphs, you set to work.
The house screamed, cried, quieted down, moaned and gagged
and lolled its split flaring tongues.
Haunted houses, you see, are very much like children
who are waiting to be fed the right spiritual candy, sweetly
everlasting
in its cherried peace.
You and the house were one,
every speck of dust doubling as starglint in your pinkest eye,
every untucked sheet awaiting your deliberate touch,
every shuttered window a warning sign,
every faded dream shadowed in storied nooks,
you, the mouse, didn't live *in* the house, you lived through it,
as one would portals, or a bloodstream, to let yourself
out meant burrowing deeper within.
So you sang, endlessly, barrowing breath into craft,
and through love's rimless labor,
showed us that stillest psalms
run deeper still.

Arclight

Jean Rhys

You held the islands in your eyes, where it rained
and rained and then the sun warmed wet to a wafting hiss.
This Jean, you, the feline slink,
filigreed shock, and sinewy comb
of white laced waves
ruffling upon
puttied blobs of shore.
Heart sore eyes,
you looked out
when no one was looking,
when the judges had lost sight of you,
and then, daring glee, you'd dive
into the smallest kingdom,
of mudpies and sandcastles,
seafizz kissing the wiggling halfmoons of fresh pink toes,
and you'd laugh and laugh, nymph of the sea,
begging its inheritance and claim
with the involuntary desperation of the meek.
Yet the islands, at the mercy of memory-tides,
flooded regularly, and you, rag doll corseted to a raft,
were carried back back back—
the shabby hotel rooms with vicious mirrors,
brightly lit cafes with trained voices
faring your terrors,
and your heart, o your poor heart,
a ruptured cadenza
consummating tender relations
with all the wrong men,
and out of its brokenness
flowed the sap and resin
or nursery school blues—
I didn't know

John Biscello

I didn't know
I didn't know.
There was the bottle, gauzy fretted palls,
the milk-fingering of wind.
There was also ribbed fringes of prose,
and that was where we found you,
alone, the barest treble,
shipwrecked on a distant island
that was mostly made of mist, and nostalgia, scabbed.
You held the islands in your eyes, Jean, where gashes
came to know the sea's suture and rhyme, its flicking blue- green tongues
as balm and frolic upon
the smallest kingdom
restored
to grace.

Arclight

Triptych (For Edie Sedgwick)

I.

Make me an offer,
they shoot pretty girls, don't they?
Leave haunting to me.

II.

Baby, forget the petals,
we'll feed you thorns,
you'll be like Jesus Christ
in black tights,
a superstar in dark eye shadow,
Joan of Arc with your own pop-branded
stigmata,
the world will adore you—
What do you say?
Will you sign?
Sure, sure, blood is fine.

III.

Too many small hours
pimped out to wraiths on parade—
Heart, in real time, breaks.

John Biscello

Dietrich in Heaven

Today I went to Heaven,
just for a brief visit.
It was a nice joint:
tangerine-fleeced runways,
and tufts of flamingo-pink
cloud, mascara-outlined,
curling softly round the edges.
There were lots of girls
there, a chorus-line of rib-sculpting
corsets, bright wigs, rouge, dark heels
like panthers, flashing sharp teeth
and puffed toes.
The brass section blared
woozy notes, as if too many dives
into the drink tank, had corrupted
the cleanest purest
Legions of their lungs
and blows.

And the smoke,
thickening Heaven,
of deep blue and ash-gray,
rose and spiraled
upupup in tight
denim streams.
Heaven, it seemed to me,
was like Berlin in the twenties.

Maybe cuz I met
the Bluest of blue angels,
Ms. Cool
freeze-frame herself,

Arclight

Marlene Dietrich.
Her voice, a pack of huskies,
after years of too-much-nightclub
smoking, pulling a sled over a slick
below-zero tundra, when she said:
Hullo, dahling. Did you bring a microphone?
The intonation of her words,
clotted peaks and dips: MICroPHOne.
No, Miss Dietrich,
can't say I did.
I was hoping
since we were in Heaven,
together, that she'd say:
Please, call me Marlene—
but she didn't.
Too bad, she said,
I was going to sing you
an old German lullaby.
I didn't want to be presumptuous,
but had to ask: Can't you sing it
without a microphone?
Deitrich's head snapped-back,
viciously, as if phantom hands had
yanked on her hair,
the punishment for an offense
she had committed
and out burst
a raspy metallic
yet buttery-smooth
in-the-center
laugh, which went on
and on, its volume
filling the whole of Heaven.
When the laughing stopped,

John Biscello

her head snapped-back to upright,
and she said: I don't know about
other women, but I require
a microphone from Earth
to sing in Heaven.
She pinched my cheek,
a little too hard.
But that's your loss, kid,
she said, her voice suddenly
taking a turn toward Bogart.
I wanted to be near Dietrich,
her ice-queenliness
making my blood run
a special kind of warm,
but I was also
scared of her, and said:
It was very nice meeting you,
Miss Dietrich, but I've got to go now.

She gingerly fingered
the ruffles,
which looked like petaled white pastries,
on her silk blouse,
and the freeze in her eyes
became daggers and knives,
cutting swiftly
into every one
of my nerve-endings.
I was paralyzed.
Dietrich's tone,
heavy cream, curdling,
when she said: Why, dahling,
donntt you lovveee me anyymmmorrre?
Without batting an eyelash,

Arclight

she wrapped both
her bare legs
around my torso, and became
a floating right-angled
vice grip, ankles twined
ribbon style, to keep me
sealed-in and barely breathing.
Far from being my introduction
to sex in heaven with Marlene Dietrich,
her legs grew longer
and longer, two smoothly shaved
and supple beanstalks,
sprouting out, vertically,
until her toes
became tiny foothills
in the distance.
Then, Dietrich parted her legs,
slightly, so I could wriggle free,
and said: Take my legs
until you can't take them anymore.
I nodded, and started walking along
Dietrich's legs, parallel tracks
that went on and on,
past the horizon,
and when I finally reached
the point where
Dietrich's legs cut off,
I fell back to Earth
hard.

John Biscello

Joan of Arc

Enlightened, perhaps. God-engorged hormones, maybe.
Regardless of why, Joan, you were the rebel prototype
long before James Dean zipped up a red jacket,
or Marlon Brando mumbled and curled his upper lip into a totem,
before Louise Brooks and Josephine Baker and Mae West
scorched bits of screen and earth and tore hearts to shreds
with a flickering edge.
You, Joan, were the world's most famous, cross-dressing heretic,
the It-girl of alleged sorcery,
a rebel very much aligned with a cause,
coursing a waxwork future and belated sainthood.

It was in your father's garden, age thirteen, when you first heard
the voices, saw the visions.
St. Michael, St. Katherine, and St. Margaret, a trinity of Beauty
unbearable that brought tears to
your eyes. But they didn't come to serve as spiritual eye-candy,
or to bring you otherworldly
comfort. They were delegates, delivering a message direct from
the Man Upstairs, a command
which, to any less a mystic, might have fallen on deaf ears, a task
that would have registered as
preposterous or impossible, but not for you Joan: faith was your
stock-in-trade.

So you listened, took it in, an illiterate, thirteen-year-old peasant
girl on the cusp of puberty,
being told that it was her duty and obligation to help lead France
to victory over the English,
to fulfill a destiny that had been part of France's prophetic
pipeline for generations: a virgin will

Arclight

come, a miracle-worker, and she will restore France to its former
glory.

You would have been happy to stay at home spinning wool with
your mother, tending to the
animals, gazing dreamily upon the milk-bearded faces of clouds,
to pass your time as a humble
girl quietly in love with God, but you knew it would be bad
form, downright impious, to argue
against a trinity of saints that had taken the time to visit you, just
you, in your father's garden.
Not to mention, when God gets in your head, like a luminous
migraine, or a marvelous tumor,
what can you do except abide?

The rest is history. Or myth. Legend. Pages from a tattered
scripture in a gilded dustbin.
Something.

There were the victories over England, the coronation of
Charles VII, at which you wielded your
iconic banner, your capture and imprisonment.

If there had been tabloids, you, Joan, would have been splashed
daily across the headlines:

France's Favorite Maid to Be Tried for Heresy
**Joan, the Teenage Witch, Refuses to Admit Allegiance to
the Devil**
Of course, as God's cheeky, chosen daughter, you had no
intention of going gently into that good
night. Several times you tried to bust out of the big house, often
falling from great heights.
When the Inquisitors grilled and viciously quizzed you with the

John Biscello

hopes of railroading you into an
incriminating confession, you shrewdly sidestepped and evaded
all their tactics, case in point:

Inquisitor: Are you in God's grace?
Joan: If I am not, may God put me there, and if I am may God
so keep me.

You had the bastards squirming, Joan, eating their own
blasphemous piles of shit.
But, as it went, they rode a gross miscarriage of justice all the
way to the stake, to that fateful
day, May 30th, 1431, when they burned you, not once, not twice,
but three times, before
scattering your ashes into the Seine.

You were nineteen. Twenty-four years away from being
acquitted at your retrial, four-hundred
and seventy-eight years away from beatification, and four-hundred and eighty-nine years away
from official sainthood.

Which just goes to show that history may be written by the
winners, but the rewrites belong to a
much higher and more mysterious order.

Arclight

Jack Kerouac

When I was a young man,
a budding scribe
eager to blossom white fire,
and scabbed lotuses,
you meant the world to me.
You exposed me to velocity bop
and piggyback rhythms,
to apple pie windowsill jazz
and summer light porch swings,
to mesmeric wreaths of pipe smoke
and the windswept skulls
of railroad Octobers
in brown, turning earth.
You soul eased
in such a relatable way,
the freight of boyhood
infused your eyes
with saloony verve,
your fingers jitterbugged
across enormous swaths of whiteness
and void,
you bootlegged
lyrics
Melville-style,
just to keep yourself
in the running with
Hemingway's bulls
and Joyce's Dublin,
white whale hunting
came second nature to you,
some people do impossible
like half-made angels

John Biscello

leveled by mortal booms.
Their very gimpness
embodies
the purest translation
of Heaven's perishable blooms.
Yours
was the religion
of sweet, sad farewells,
the capered goofs
of little boys spitballing
I love yous
to girls in pinafore dresses
at Sunday movie matinees,
or profane leerstruckness
at the silver crucifixes
resting
between ripening mounds
of sweat beaded cleavage,
yours
was the racket of vaudeville,
commingled with a fanatic's
fairground zeal,
the Zen weatherman
who once proclaimed:
The taste
of rain—
why kneel?
Yet
it wasn't long
before
Fame,
that highly-sought-after
stalk-legged
dame

Arclight

in a mink stole
and white-hot spray
of jewels
came along
and cornered you good,
and the Shakespeare of Lowell
quickly became
Little Boy Blue,
nowhere to turn,
as the flesh eaters
closed in,
and all you could do
was blow wild, careening
solos through your trusty horn,
and pour
rivers of whiskey
over your soul's
god given.
Recognition didn't kill you,
alcoholism did,
but let's just say
recognition
mixed with booze
in the redlight district
and pinkened sensitivity
of wounded souls
sharpens
and humors itself
through the gallows.
When names
balloon too big,
when the print is lettered
through the Hypemachine,
it is easy

John Biscello

to lose sight
of what it is we're reading,
Fame's overlay
the distorting veneer
so you are no longer reading
what you see or feel
but rather what you've heard
from a hivemind,
secondhand rumors dispel
direct engagement with mystery,
what others know
and say
becomes the order of the day,
and that long day's journey
into night
is, by definition
and default, history
(its winners wearing blinders
while leading the blind)
but before the siege,
and after the deluge,
Jack Kerouac, Ti Jean, Sal Paradise, John Duluouz,
and all the other names that became you,
there were the words, the holy writ,
the godblasted scrolls of one man's
self-speak upon the earth,
that rabid seeking
as gilded sibling
to Dylan Thomas's hilltop cloud cry—
Oh, as I was young once,
and easy in the mercy of his means,
Time held me green and dying,
Though I sang in my chains like the sea.
You,

Arclight

Mr. Kerouac,
were one of the wind-twisting
chain-rattlers,
frothing fringed baubles of sea
at the mouth,
as if to prove
you were nature herself
(this the way of angels, the way of children)
and when I look back,
I am immensely grateful
that you took the time
to give the spirit of boyhood,
its vim and keyturned sorcery,
as well as music's
plasmic alchemy,
its reverential due
in a society
where doped dreams
register
way too much sleep
to ever claim their meek
as soundly vital
and golden.

John Fante

Inferiority might have been your first memory.
Though you were born on American soil,
Denver, CO, April 8th, 1909,
the chinked chains of immigration
had you by the throat and bowels, pinched your nerves
as you butted your head against the scabby base of a totem pole.
You, the little wop, the fenced-in dago, trying to dig his way
to China, or the moon, or to any form of greatness
that would eclipse your undermining complexes.
And so, out of shame and need, out of fevered desire,
you created Bandini, or he you.
Arturo Bandini, rising star and literary godsend
of John Fante's complicated inner world,
soon to be exported and appraised and adored
by thousands, maybe more.
Arturo Bandini would draw from your history
and chagrin—your philandering, boozing, gambling father,
your mother, having to beg credit to keep the family fed,
your fear and loathing of Jesus,
and love-hate relations with the saints,
all of it would fuel Bandini's quest
to transcend your blues,
your gnawing sense of lesser-than.
You would become the Joe DiMaggio of the literary world,
the gold-plated pride and joy of your people,
or at least go down swinging.
Bandini, fire in his belly, lean days of determination,
a starved mongrel digesting the pit and seeds
and citrus rinds and sun-tendered leaves
of palm trees in 1930s L.A., an angry, confused, passionate
young man, stalking fury and sound, full of himself
and words that he prayed to God would not let him down.

Arclight

He, John Fante, the great Arturo Bandini, gave us pages,
a score of scorched pages, not enough according to him
(he would go on to become a Hollywood screenwriter
and malign himself as the worst kind of traitor to his soul and calling)
but he left behind the Bandini Quartet, four novels
with his grit-infused masterpiece, *Ask the Dust*, forming its apex.
Some angry young men mellow with age,
Fante, it seems, raged until the end.
His legs, and sight, were claimed by diabetes,
and Fante, as a blind amputee, bed-ridden, took one last dive
and salutary fling into the inspired world of Bandini,
dictating his final novel, *Dreams from Bunker Hill*, to his wife, Joyce.
Bukowski, who had accidentally stumbled upon Fante's work,
considered him a god.
The two would become friends, and Bukowki would do his part
to resurrect Fante for a new generation.
It seems, after all, that Bandini, upon a cross,
grinning, scowling, dreaming of words
and how to arrange them according to gospel,
had amounted to a scarring glint
upon so much favored dust.

John Biscello

Henry Miller

Some men rattle their chains and wonder, some sing them.
Then there are others who spray paint their chains rainbow siege
and dance a jig like a peacock on fire, and when someone asks
Isn't it hard to dance around with those chains weighing you down,
the man laughs heartily and responds—What chains, my dear lad,
these are feathers. Listen to the way they jangle and clink when I dance,
have you ever heard feathers that sound like that? Miraculous and unusual, yes?
You, Henry Miller, were one of those men.
You turned wrought-iron links, Brooklyn-made, into loafer's foam,
into dreamfaring plumage, unabashed in its frisson and vainglory,
smeared bottom's up in in deep semen envy, angel's spit, and stolen honey.
Vagabondage was your claim, but not your master.
Though you did have many teachers—bilious clowns, crowded streets,
torn trousers, children's capered faces, gateless barbarians,
your mother's frigid ruler (and how you learned the only thing
worth measuring was love, that which belonged to the immeasurable).
A lusty little scamp at heart, eyes unpopping buttons
and sailing seas of skirts in parks, you were literature's answer to Charlie Chaplin,
with an unzipped mouth and cracked tower of seismic songs to yawp,
the world needed a Henry Miller, because you said so,
and in cement that remained eternally wet, you signed your

Arclight

name
and sang, Whitmanesque, of yourself, again and again and again,
an explodingly insistent echo,
and the sincerest of forgeries,
because, for those dwelling between lines,
a signature verifying an identity—
I am he, he is me, he is he, I am I, etc.,
never does true justice
to the multitudinous at work
in the playing of one's self as instrument
upon which God's deep welling nothingness
meets and mates with one's youthingness,
and from there, bang.
Just bang and wow and let's make radical inscrutable love,
music, art, whatever.
You, "Henry Miller," wink-wink,
gave us your pulsing timepiece of whatever,
and you, Henry Miller, as my Brooklyn soul-chum and compatriot,
separated by age but not spirit,
granted me amnesty
and helped me to unlock my own
bang, wow, and whatever
resounding yes
whatever
yes
yes.

John Biscello

The Horse's Mouth (for Dylan Thomas)

And all the piper's children will swim
the sea's misaligned symmetry,
where crested upon a wave,
about to buckle,
that wild mane of curly locks—
kinked tresses
tossed by a trident, cross,
and sudsalty tears.

Now, Thomas, who's doubting
that off the Horse
your Fall from a stool
would resound in Heaven?

A loss is a loss, of course,
and from the trough the Gift Horse
feeds on paper-thin straw.
Yet,
Death's goodnight,
whether gentle as a cotton kiss,
or unrepentantly rough,
will not shut you up:
so you answer my poem in quizzical morse code:
Am I not the charmed sorcerer
made to spin straw into gold?
Am I not 18 whiskies
away from some sort of
corner-turned Eternity?

Locks, braggadocio,
and lyrical lilt aside,
I say rest now,

Arclight

rest well knowing
your sheaf of spindly myths
have rooted and out sprouted
a series of stately trees...
and not a single branch is bare of birdsong.

When alive
                and shouldering a mountain's sea of salt,
bone and blade gritted together,
friction-forging wings,
singed,
                inciting the burning bird to sing
of horizons to come.

The mind on fire
in its toil and hum,
cast curses
givin birth to excursions
convertin boils to storm.

All in all bricks in the wall,
but the horse, dreaming itself a strange bird,
turned flights of fancy
into racing against the grain—
handicap rail-splittin the odds
into breaks:
                the heart's hiccupped bluff and puff
and skip and scratch
                bring it back
bluff and puff and skip and scratch—
repeat action tracked
to the belief
that just beyond the wall
lay a relief route doubling as a refuge.

John Biscello

Fear not, Thomas, you doubting fool
and swindler savant,
for poetry's High Court of Judges
gavel-slammin the verdict:
>> Guilty,
>> of sentimental excess,
>> Guilty,
>> of verses cryptic, obscene, and lacking
>> coherence,
>> Guilty,
>> of gifts god-given soiled and neglected—
can no longer lay siege to the pink of your ears
and easy-to-bruise-blue-Ego.

Blessed be death's deafness
to shouldacouldawouldabeen
criticisms and bonepicks—
meaning means nil
when what you gave
is all the matter we've got
on record
in a soundproofed safe for the ages.

It is common knowledge
that all the piper's children
and king's horses
splash frantically in the end—
last-gasp ravenous for one more song,
a barstool ditty or
sea-conched choral,
just one more song
so as not to serenade the setting sun
on an unmade deathbed,
regretfully saying: "After 39 years, this is all I've done."

Arclight

It is time to rest, Thomas.
The horse is dead,
its head cut off and flung to the sea,
undertow tagging its gift mouth,
which continues to shout forget-me-nots
in dramatic Welsh baritone.

It is time for one last tip a the glass, Thomas,
a toast to you and your Wumblyworld menagerie of horses,
birds,
cripples, perverts, lovers and milk maidens:
here's hopin
Heaven does indeed
reserve a section for boyhood
everlasting.

Lighted Proof

John Biscello

Intraverse, Epitaph for a Beginning

1.

Bidden by tatters, and gravity's mutable arc, the palpitations guide me.
They are subtle, duly engaged, a milk-slow run of shivers.
Bracing the rim, I peer out of cavedark: everything is sudden,
color-soaked, a ferocious din and melt,
fringed shawls of plasma groped by wind.
My eyes struggle to adjust.
At first they all seem like vagrant stabs of light, undifferentiated,
and then comes the exact piercing, prayer of motherlight
warming my lungs,
as if I've swallowed a blush.
I realize, with grave tenderness, that I am being born of this
split,
the heir and progeny of absence.
Hers, his: a recursive lineage of fractures.
Ready or not, my history is formed, my destiny fixed—
I am a furious comeback waiting to happen.

2.

She swallows stones,
or is made to—what feels
like a martyred plunge of boulders.
I am, by proxy, crushed.
Is this what is meant by god-dam?
The circulatory flush of light
to dark dammed, and no god gets
in or out, what amounts to a gag order
or mouthless idol
claiming little to no

Arclight

real value?

3.

One of the Echoes stated
that being born is like
drawing silence from blood.
True? False? I cannot tell.
The Echoes resound everywhere,
choral flocks spanning the spectrum
from roar to hush; they are
the vocabulary I have inherited,
as if by default.

4.

It's hard to gauge with finite
accuracy, but I am aware—
she is growing and I am not.
It is, I suspect,
in my nature
to remain small and wanting,
a grievous flutter or
remote hint
cusping revelation.

5.

I get so sleepy
and restless
and roiled
and charged.
If only they knew
what they called *world*

was simply a clusterfuck
of particles
dreaming of dance partners.

6.

It is both pleasure, and an epitaph to pleasure,
at the same time.
When the phenomena occurs
and the colors run
and slash
and slit down upon me
in ravels of deluge.
Spring-green, shell-pink, sky-blue,
bled-red, egg-heaven, grief-yellow.
I, a perpetual guest
bearing witness
to my own seeds
and desires,
feel at home,
happy prey to a luminous gust,
when the colors cake
and blast through me.
It is then that I no longer fear dry clefted
hollows, or loud leveling booms.
It is lighted proof
that I am not forgotten.

7.

There are no mirrors here,
yet everywhere I see myself,
a bated draft of furls,
each bearing the right

Arclight

to exist, and respire ably.

8.

I have found
that the impeccable masks
she carves and wears out
with devotional vigor
place me at risk.
By varying turns
and degrees, Intimacy, braised,
grows more distant and endangered
and I with it.
How to stay her hand, or reverse charged currents?
I have tried consulting with the Echoes,
but that was like spitting into bundles of rain,
each droplet anonymous in its gospel
and creed.

9.

They count the age
with linear tact,
enabling stricture.
I do not get this.
The digits do not run
static in a fixed course,
they are not soldiers lined up single-file
marching toward common oblivion.
Age bears shoots and novelty, functions in multiples.
You are not six only once,
nor are you exclusively 33
when you come to exist in your thirty-third year.
Age, in its cumulative front,

is amorphous and inherently radical,
its autonomy breaches named conditions
and numbered plots.
Six happens at six,
and at nine, and at seventeen,
and thirty-three, and so on,
its claim contingent upon variables.
And I, sclerotic
in the cradle of a false womb,
cannot be held or christened by age;
there is no past or future, no number or given name,
for the fates annulled
at childhood's edge.

10.

Blue sparks, candles, dancing eyes, bright bulbs of gabble and
noise, flung garlands of prayer—
today she is seventeen.
Lipsticked, flaps of scent, strong legs, rogue piercings, pageboy
cut, black pumps, gallery of masks
and knives—
today she enters seventeen, acid and armed to the teeth,
and I, binding coil,
wait in the wings.

11.

In becoming a ghost
to my own medium,
I am drifting toward clemency,
toward the solvency of locks.
The Echoes, of course, refute this,
and in stereo.

Arclight

They assure me
that no matter how far the drift,
no matter how deep the cleave,
playing ghost
to my own dream of living
is just another slant of haunt
masquerading as exorcism.
A conundrum, with no respite,
I am baffled by the source of the Echoes, and wonder—
Is there more to me than her?
Where exactly do I begin, and end?
Would I cast a shadow upon a wall in a world without?
I continue to drift, unanswered.

12.

I have begun to name and catalogue the different types of dark.
It helps.
Warm-dark, cave-dark, void-dark, womb-dark, sleep-dark,
Eros-dark, blank-dark, siege-dark,
and there is the anonymous dark that gets in your head
and behind your eyes and in your lungs and constricts your breathing;
curse-dark, which casts a heavy prolonged spell, a pall;
there is also lonely. Naming it doesn't help, not in the same way.

13.

Gnashing, teething, bristling, ranting, raving—
all, in this momentary wreck, becomes black with tumult.
It is the dark I forgot to name.

John Biscello

14.

Wafting from afar,
the intimate rumor of a divine toy,
a cryptic plaything, implications in tow.
A tonic
and pacifier of blank rages;
buoy and anti-freeze
to sudden plunges
into sub-zero climate.
These conditions cannot be bested,
but they can be met.
If, and here's where pressure takes root,
if we were in possession of this divine toy,
this cryptic plaything, which may only be
the waning flicker of legend, of evidence withheld.

15.

Seized, I am in the ripe
feral grip of the new language
she is speaking. Her voice
fronting a glassy, ciphered edge, a grifting menace.
Every calculated utterance bears double and triple meaning, with
common intent to baffle,
disarm, intrigue, estrange; a misleading
skein of confession.
In a sense, her unwitting compulsion
to protect me is the root-cause of her
language, its architecture and vents.
If only she could
abide the silence long enough to exact
the necessary vigil;
if only she didn't consign

Arclight

my pink to arson.

16.

To become more or less
human, and right now I am less,
much less, palsied, unlit, a compulsory golem
riveting shallows and depths.

17.

It came to me, a pensive glean, a vision.
Tomorrowtime when we, the Inners, will no longer just be metaphysical whispers
or codified concepts.
Tomorrowtime when the Outers will have found the means to extrapolate us,
to call us into the world of appetite and elemental yen
(e.g., how light and air cherish in unison).
We will gather as gnostic rumors confirmed as true.
Our caretakers will be directly confronted by the gestalt of our lives,
by our stasis and afflictions.
Brood to their former distances, they will grow nearer to us;
they will live as bright apologies to our scars;
they will sorrow for a long, long spell, every last fracture recalling its grief;
and we, barrowing the course of right rain, will come to master how light and air cherish in unison.

18.

So much light
poured in,

John Biscello

so much
passive worth.

19.

Today, today, today, today, today, today,
this drumbeat I sometimes try and divide into equal sections and measures.
Yet it is like swimming across an encyclopedia
of sea to vet and speciously catalog
rounds of waves—this one this, this one that;
continuity of a jaded gag.

20.

Blindly, blindly, blindly,
she reaps every choice
from my scythe and asking.
I live with brute innocence
and murder in her heart.
I am not her child,
I am her fiction,
her sad fable
and paling wrath.

21.

   1. Honeymoon, forever, ballad, veil, bond, forever again—I am
      caving beneath terms that she is repeatedly packing into the hollows.
      It is a new kind of spell, whorling and vestal.

   2. Perhaps it is the wrong kind of spell,

Arclight

        not to be trusted.

3. The words, as aural emblems, became real.
   She, in bright ceremony, matched her absences,
   with fidelity and crux, to someone else's.
   Honeymoon, forever, ballad, veil, bond, forever again;
   my language has become canticle
   to a lighted theme.

4. She is flush and expectant with dream,
   and together we tumble toward
   an impossible arc.
   Story-dark. I have named a new one.

5. The hollows flood
   and brim with a wheeling geometry
   of vibrant colors
   in which I bathe.

6. When gesture and symmetry
   become one and the same,
   Intimacy is moved
   to daring.

7. I listen to them talk,
   like tolling vespers,
   like a warm robe of sound
   in which I nestle
   and chasten.

8. The days lean against each other,
   a staggered verisimilitude.
   The ennobling of Legacy

has fast become
a dependency of tatters
and shrieks.

9. Honeymoon, forever, ballad, veil, bond, forever
   again—
   Map to her old scars,
   I pitch these words,
   void of testament,
   into a smoldering hollow;
   what the flames don't devour,
   the Echoes will scavenge.

22.

The cited erring
of will and bones,
she has taken leave
of Memory to become
a spectacle of caution.
Rote, exacting, severe,
everything in its place, just so,
to enable function,
and I, the feathery cringe
at the bottom of her fear,
am held, with contempt,
to the highest standard.

23.

In a vain attempt,
she corseted herself in green wind
and cellophane, votives
to a thin whip of air.

Arclight

As she lay there,
colors emptying to gray,
before the round voices
and fast hands came,
she fell in
and saw me for the first time,
not as fiction or sad fable,
but as a soiled fact
that had been abandoned to peril.
Every last knife and mask slowed to weeping,
venting a silvery glean.

24.

There is an epitaph marking
the life we have lived
from the ones we have not.
This is where I begin
to separate the words
from their cause,
running on, unfinished,
end to start.

ABOUT THE AUTHOR

Originally from Brooklyn, NY, author, poet, playwright and performer, John Biscello has lived in Taos, NM since 2001. He is the author of three novels—*Broken Land, a Brooklyn Tale, Raking the Dust,* and *Nocturne Variations*—and a collection of short stories, *Freeze Tag*. His adaptations of classic fables were paired with the vintage illustrations of Paul Bransom, in the children's book—*Once Upon A Time: Classic Fables Reimagined*. His poetry and fiction has appeared in: Art Times, nthposition, Ophelia Street, The Wanderlust Review, The Iconoclast, Adobe Walls, Kansas City Voices, The Tishman Review, and numerous other journals and zines. *Arclight* is his debut poetry collection.

His novels are available through Unsolicited Press (unsolicitedpress.com), Amazon, and other outlets.

Blog/website:
johnbiscello.com

Amazon author page:
https://www.amazon.com/John-Biscello/e/B008987E40

www.ingramcontent.com/pod-product-compliance
Lightning Source LLC
Chambersburg PA
CBHW030329080526
44584CB00012B/779